Ellen Ochoa

Breaking Barriers in Space

by Jennifer Marino Walters
illustrated by Scott R. Brooks

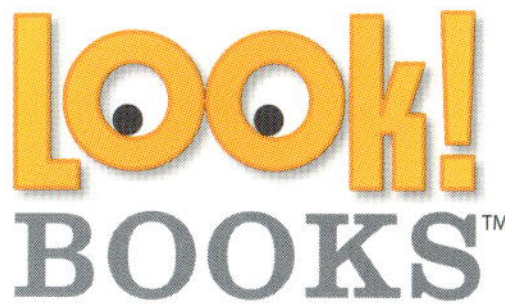

Red Chair Press   Egremont, Massachusetts

Look! Books are produced and published by Red Chair Press:

Red Chair Press LLC   PO Box 333   South Egremont, MA 01258-0333

www.redchairpress.com

 FREE lesson guide at www.redchairpress.com/free-activities

Publisher's Cataloging-In-Publication Data
(Provided by Cassidy Cataloguing Services, Inc.)
Names: Marino Walters, Jennifer, author. | Brooks, Scott R., illustrator.
Title: Ellen Ochoa : breaking barriers in space / by Jennifer Marino Walters ;
illustrated by Scott R. Brooks.

Other titles: Look! books (Red Chair Press). Beginner biography

Description: Egremont, Massachusetts : Red Chair Press, [2024] | Includes
index. | Interest age level: 006-009. | Summary: Ellen Ochoa was selected
by NASA in 1990 to join its astronaut program, and she became the first
Hispanic female astronaut when she completed her training in 1991. Two
years later she flew on the space shuttle Discovery, becoming the first
Latina to be launched into space. Ochoa continued breaking barriers at
NASA for women and for Hispanics.--Publisher.

Identifiers: ISBN: 9781643712505 (library hardcover) | 9781643712567
(softcover) | 9781643712628 (ebook) | LCCN: 2022943824

Subjects: LCSH: Ochoa, Ellen--Juvenile literature. | Hispanic American
astronauts--Biography--Juvenile literature. | Women astronauts--United
States--Biography--Juvenile literature. | CYAC: Ochoa, Ellen. | Hispanic
American astronauts--Biography. | Women astronauts--United States--
Biography. | LCGFT: Biographies. | BISAC: JUVENILE NONFICTION
/ Biography & Autobiography / Women. | JUVENILE NONFICTION /
Science & Nature / Astronomy. | JUVENILE NONFICTION / People &
Places / United States / Hispanic & Latino.

Classification: LCC: TL789.85.O25 M37 2024 | DDC: 629.450092--dc23

Photo credits: NASA

Printed in the United States of America

0324 1P CGF24

Table of Contents

California Childhood

Ellen Ochoa was born on May 10, 1958 in Los Angeles, California. Her parents were from the United States and her father's parents (her grandparents) were from Mexico.

Ellen's family moved to La Mesa, a suburb of San Diego. Ellen grew up there as the middle child of five brothers and sisters.

Young Scholar

Ellen's parents split up when she was a teenager. She and her siblings lived with their mother. Ellen's mother taught them that school was very important.

Ellen listened carefully. She worked hard and got very good grades. She loved math and playing the flute.

When Ellen got to college, she planned to study music. Instead, she decided to study physics. Physics is the science of how **matter** and energy affect each other.

After college, Ellen went to another university to study engineering. Engineering is the science of developing and using nature's power and **resources** in ways that are useful to people.

Ellen chose to go to San Diego State University to be close to her family. She graduated in 1980 and then attended Stanford University to study engineering, where she earned her highest degree in 1985.

Hard Work

In 1988, Ellen joined the National **Aeronautics** and Space Administration (NASA) as a research engineer. She decided she wanted to be an astronaut. The first two times she applied to be one, NASA said no.

But Ellen did not give up. She
worked hard at her job. She
invented new devices that work
with light. She even learned to
fly an airplane.

Making History

In 1990, Ellen applied to be an astronaut again. This time, she got the job! Ellen joined NASA's Johnson Space Center in Texas, where she trained to go to space.

In April 1993, Ellen made history. She became the first Hispanic woman ever to go to space. Ellen flew with four other astronauts aboard the Space Shuttle *Discovery*. The mission lasted nine days.

Discovery
NASA

After that, Ellen went to space three more times in 1994, 1999, and 2002. In all, she spent nearly 1,000 hours in **orbit**.

Ellen performed many tasks in space. She operated a robotic arm to place **satellites** into orbit. She did science experiments. She worked on the International Space Station (ISS), a laboratory in space. She even exercised and played the flute while in space.

Good to Know

The first American woman to ever go to space was Sally Ride. She flew aboard the Space Shuttle *Challenger* on June 18, 1983.

Back on Earth

After her last trip to space, Ellen remained at the Johnson Space Center. There, she helped support space exploration from Earth.

In 2013, Ellen became the Johnson Space Center's first Hispanic director. She held that job for five years before retiring from NASA in 2018.

JAXA
VVO
17

Big Honors

Ellen has received many awards for her work. These include NASA's highest award, the Distinguished Service Medal.

In 2017, Ellen was **inducted** into the U.S. Astronaut Hall of Fame. She also has six schools named after her in California, Oklahoma, Washington, and Texas.

U.S. ASTRONAUT
HALL OF FAME
2017 INDUCTEES
ELLEN OCHOA
NASA

ASTRONAUT
SCHOLARSHIP
FOUNDATION

Delaware
North.

Kennedy
Space Center
VISITOR COMPLEX

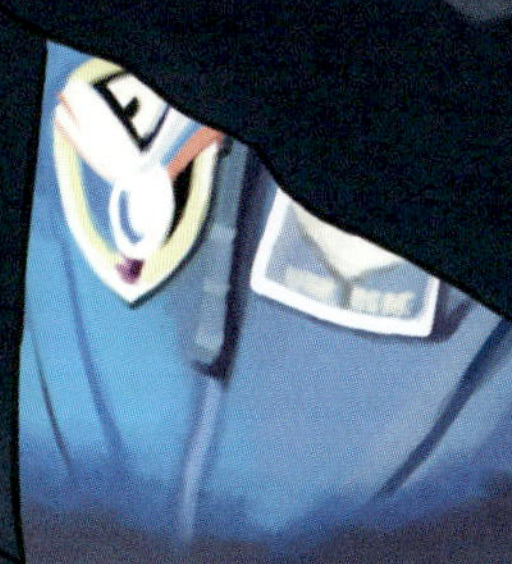

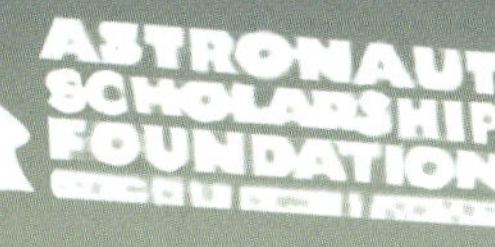

19

Inspiring Others

Ellen loves to share her experiences with kids across the U.S. She has given hundreds of talks on the importance of a STEM (science, technology, engineering, and math) education.

Ellen hopes to inspire women and people of all backgrounds to work in STEM jobs, and even to become astronauts. She knows if she could do it, anyone can!

NASA

Timeline: Big Dates in Ellen's Life

1958: Ellen is born in Los Angeles, California.

1980: Ellen graduates from San Diego State University; enrolls at Stanford University for Engineering studies.

1988: She joins NASA as a research engineer.

1990: Ellen is accepted into NASA's astronaut training program. She marries husband Coe Miles.

1993: Ellen becomes the first Hispanic woman to go to space.

1994–2002: She goes to space three more times, spending nearly 1,000 hours in orbit.

2013: Ellen becomes the Johnson Space Center's first Hispanic director.

2015: She receives NASA's highest award, the Distinguished Service Medal.

2017: Ellen is inducted into the U.S. Astronaut Hall of Fame.

2018: She retires from NASA after a 30-year career.

2020: Ellen becomes Chair of the National Science Board.

Words to Know

aeronautics: the science of flight

inducted: placed into

matter: anything that takes up space

orbit: the curved path that something (such as a space shuttle) follows as it goes around something else (like a planet)

resources: things that can be used

satellites: machines in space that orbit a planet, the moon, or the sun

Learn More at the Library

(Check out these books to read with others)

Kittinger, Jo S. *The Astronaut With a Song for the Stars.* The Innovation Press, 2019.

Jaffe, Elizabeth D. *Ellen Ochoa.* Children's Press, 2005.

Schwartz, Heather E. *Astronaut Ellen Ochoa.* Lerner Classroom, 2017.

Index

About the Author

Jennifer Marino Walters has never been to space. But she and her husband with their twin boys and daughter have looked for the International Space Station in the Washington D.C. area night skies where she lives and works.